BECOMING AN IMPACTFUL YOUTH

7 Outstanding Attributes to Have

Temitope A. Oshin

Independently published

Copyright © 2026 Temitope A. Oshin

All rights reserved

No part of this book may be reproduced, or stored in a retrieval system, or transmitted in any form or by any means, electronic, mechanical, photocopying, recording, or otherwise, without express written permission of the publisher.

info@wholeteensministries.ng

Unless otherwise stated, quoted Scripture are taken from the New King James Version®. Copyright © 1982 by Thomas Nelson. Used by permission. All rights reserved.

ISBN: 9798241504944

Cover design by:
Library of Congress Control Number:
Printed in the United States of America

This work is dedicated
"To God my Exceeding Joy" (Psalm 43:4)
"My Father ... the Guide of my youth" (Jeremiah 3:4)

CONTENTS

Title Page

Copyright

Dedication

Introduction   1

Chapter One   6

Chapter Two   9

Chapter Three   13

Chapter Four   20

Chapter Five   28

Chapter Six   31

Chapter Seven   34

About The Author   37

Books By This Author   39

INTRODUCTION

"Rejoice, O young man, in your youth, and let your heart cheer you in the days of your youth…"
(Ecclesiastes 11:9)

Every developed society thrives on the strength of its youths. Mighty nations attain greatness on the account of the viability of their youthful demographics. Productivity, prosperity and profitability are the direct results of an engaged and industrious youthful population of a nation. Youths are indispensable to the advancement of a nation. The youths in their numbers are makers and movers of development; in their strengths, they are the shakers and shovers of advancement. Mighty in numbers, great in strength; that's the power of the youth!

The tragedy of any society is the lack or laxity of its youths. A youthful population which is not useful to its society is like a gem thrown into the sea. As a young person, you are meant to be the pride of your family and the glory of your nation. Most importantly, you are loved by God and you are meant to be His useful ambassadors. It is not enough to just be youthful, it is more impactful to be useful. Being youthful has its attendant blessings and advantages, but committing to be useful as a youth for God, your nation and your family, comes with unfathomable rewards and eternal blessings.

Youth is one of the most powerful seasons of life. It is a season filled with strength, curiosity, vision, and limitless potential. It is a time when dreams are formed, destinies are shaped, and foundations for the future are laid. Yet, it is also a season that can be easily wasted, misdirected, or misunderstood.

Every generation rises or falls on the strength, direction, and character of its youth. Nations are built or broken by them. Families are preserved or weakened through them. The future of society rests heavily on how well young people discover purpose, embrace responsibility, and align their lives with truth.

This book was written with you in mind — the young person who desires more than survival, popularity, or temporary success. It is for those who hunger for meaning, impact, and lasting relevance. It is for those who desire to live a life that counts — not just for today, but for eternity.

Being young is a privilege, but being useful is a choice.

Many youths possess energy, talent, and ambition, yet lack direction, discipline, or divine guidance. Strength without purpose can lead to frustration. Passion without wisdom can lead to destruction. Talent without character can ruin destinies. This book exists to help you avoid these pitfalls and to guide you toward a life of purpose, balance, and godly impact.

The truth is this: God has invested something powerful inside you. You are not an accident of time or chance. You were created with intention, gifted with potential, and designed to make a difference in your generation.

The Bible clearly reveals that youthfulness is not a limitation but an advantage. Scripture celebrates the strength, passion, creativity, and vision that characterize the young. It affirms that young people can walk in wisdom, lead with courage, and influence their world for good. Throughout Scripture, God repeatedly entrusted great assignments to young men and women who were willing, available, and obedient.

This book draws from that Biblical truth.

What This Book Is About

Becoming an Impactful Youth explores seven foundational attributes that shape young people into instruments of positive influence. These attributes are drawn from Scripture and illustrated through timeless biblical principles that remain relevant across cultures, generations, and continents.

Each chapter focuses on one essential attribute:

- **Vigour** – Harnessing your strength for meaningful pursuits
- **Vision** – Seeing beyond now into God's purpose
- **Virtue** – Building character that sustains success
- **Values** – Establishing unshakable moral foundations
- **Verve** – Living with passion, enthusiasm, and spiritual fire
- **Valour** – Walking in courage despite fear or opposition
- **Visible Impact** – Leaving a tangible mark on your world

Together, these attributes form a blueprint for a life that glorifies God and blesses humanity.

Who This Book Is For

This book is for:

- Young people seeking clarity about their purpose
- Students navigating identity, pressure, and direction

- Youth leaders, mentors, and pastors guiding the next generation

- Anyone desiring to live intentionally and make lasting impact

Whether you are in your teens, twenties, or early thirties — or simply young at heart — this book will challenge, inspire, and guide you toward a life of significance.

How to Use This Book

This is not a book to rush through. It is designed to be:

- Read prayerfully

- Reflected upon deeply

- Applied practically

At the end of each chapter, pause and reflect. Ask yourself honest questions. Pray. Journal. Discuss with others if possible. Transformation does not come from information alone but from application.

A Call to Action

The world is waiting for a generation of young people who will rise with clarity, conviction, and courage. A generation that will not conform to decay but will become agents of renewal. A generation that will shine as light in dark places.

You are not too young to make a difference.

You are not too small to be significant.

You are not too weak to be used by God.

Your journey toward impact begins now.

Welcome to a life of purpose.

Welcome to a life of influence.

Welcome to *Becoming an Impactful Youth*.

CHAPTER ONE
Attribute #1: Vigour

"The glory of young men is their strength..."
(Proverbs 20:29)

One of the most obvious attributes of the youth is vigour or strength. Strength in the youth reveals itself in the physical vigour with which tasks are carried out and the spiritual vitality with which Godly pursuits are followed. Young people are known for their energy and drive. An average young person is full of life and vitality. They are ready to undertake tasks, no matter how daunting, and are adventurous.

This key attribute manifests itself in both the good and the bad. When not properly channelled, youthful energy and strength can be expended in the pursuit of ill-motivated endeavours. This is why the youth needs guidance, positive direction and Godly counsel. Today, several young people are in passionate and energetic pursuit of unscrupulous missions aimed at gaining quick wealth, sudden fame and popularity. You must desist from such negative and wasteful discharge of your God-given vigour and strength. The Bible tells us that the glory of youths is their strength. Use your strength, energy and vigour for things that bring glory to God. Let your pursuits in life be Godly and glorifying; and channel your vigour to attain them.

Are you hungry for a life of meaningful impact? Do you seek to see your generation changed for God? Are you driven by the quest to see others transformed to become the best they can be? You are not alone. These things are the pursuits of Christian youths who have encountered the saving grace of our Lord Jesus Christ. They are driven, fuelled and propelled by the energy of the Holy Spirit to affect their world and make it a better place. You too can channel the strength God has given you to such positive endeavours. But first things first. You must put your faith and trust in the Lord Jesus Christ. You need Him to realign your values, transform your mind and make you a shining light. You have a chance to do things right and go after the right things, right now. Pray now and ask Jesus to come into your heart and make you one of His own useful youths.

Dear friend, your strength and vigour as a youth is vital to God. He needs you to accomplish great, good and glorious tasks for Him. You need to be prepared to be a useful youth in the hands of your Creator. Keep your energy up; keep your drive pumped; let your strength not wane. Keep your spirit high; your vigour is your channel to great accomplishments.

It is not uncommon to have times and seasons when young people go weary and exhausted in their pursuits. The Bible tells us that:

> *"Even the youths shall faint and be weary...but those who wait on the LORD shall renew their strength; they shall mount up with wings like eagles, they shall run and not be weary, they shall walk and not faint."* (Isaiah 40: 30, 31)

At such times, the Bible recommends the solution is to "wait on the LORD". As a Christian youth, when you feel weak in your walk with God, you don't have to give up. When you feel exhausted, what you have to do is keep walking in the faith and wait on the LORD for renewed strength and fervour. We can learn from the example of Gideon and his companions. Though exhausted at the point of crossing the Jordan, the Bible says they "crossed over, exhausted but still in pursuit." (Judges 8:4).

Who can help return your lost strength and spiritual vitality? Who can help restore your broken relationship with God? The Bible says:

> *"Have you not known?*
> *Have you not heard?*
> *The Everlasting God, the LORD,*
> *The Creator of the ends of the earth,*
> *Neither faints nor is weary.*
> *His understanding is unsearchable.*
> *He gives power to the weak,*
> *And to those who have no might He increases strength."*
> (Isaiah 40: 28, 29)

Do you feel weak and exhausted in your pursuits in life? Are you discouraged because of past failures and disappointments? Has your inner drive and energy waned? This is the time to reach out to God for a renewed strength. God is All you need. He gives power to the weak and to those who have no might He increases strength. Reach out to your Creator and Father, He will revive you and strengthen your feeble knees for an invigorating pursuit of your life goals. Wait on the Lord!

CHAPTER TWO
Attribute #2: Vision

"Your young men shall see visions..."
(Acts 2:17)

Another key attribute of the youth is their ability to see visions. Visions characterize the youthful season of life. By vision, I mean the grace to conceptualize ideas, mental pictures of a glorious future, aspirations of a colourful life and the blueprint of a better tomorrow. Youths are uniquely predisposed to conceive visions or dreams. They possess the God-given grace to see possibilities and opportunities beyond what ordinarily the present holds. They see beyond today, the great achievements destined for tomorrow. Every young person is crafted like that. Even the old people dream dreams, according to Acts 2:17, why won't the young see visions too? God is gracious in the way he fashioned us as humans, we have the ability to dream or desire good things which are yet to materialize. That ability is especially at its peak as a young person when life is beginning and promising with potential.

Most of the great tasks I do now as an adult, I had conceived them as a teenager beaming with the life of God. I find that true for most great achievers I know too. Joseph dreamt of his glorious future as a teenager (Genesis 37:2,5,9). God gave him the blueprint of his assignment and the glory of its fulfilment while he was still a youth. David caught a glimpse of his royal assignment while he was a shepherd boy in his teen years.

You too must have had some bright ideas about what you want to do in the future. Your youthful season is a season of discovery. Latent gifts and talents begin to show as you grow into adolescence through to your teenage years, they even become more evident as you become a young adult.

As a young person, you are filled with a possibility attitude, you just dream and dream, not knowing how or whether those dreams will come to pass. Your youthful innocence and innate strengths form a unique alliance that keeps you positive about your future irrespective of what your present social status or conditions may be. You discover how good you are at writing, or singing, or drawing, or painting, or dancing or playing a musical instrument, or teaching, or speaking, or running, or at sports (the list is endless). This discovery makes you conceive great ideas about what you wish to become or do later in life. Am I striking a chord?

The next thing any great vision or dream compels the visionary or dreamer to do is to document it. The Bible says:

> *"Write the vision*
> *And make it plain on tablets,*
> *That he may run who reads it."*
> *(Habakkuk 2:2)*

Writing down your vision and dream gives you the first sign of confidence that it is possible to achieve. Faith builds up in you when you see continually, from penning down, what you have first seen or conceived in your mind. Writing down your vision ensures you do not lose sight of it with passing time. Rather, it magnifies your mental picture of the vision and makes it all the more clearer day by day. Another thing writing down your vision does is that it helps you draw up a workable plan for its achievement. "Write the vision…that he may run who reads it". Document your great ideas. Think on paper. However, don't just stop there, act on them!

Remember, every vision has an appointed time. If you don't document it and devise a plan for it, when the appointed time comes, it might meet you unprepared. The Bible says:

> *"For the vision is yet for an appointed time;*
> *But at the end it will speak, and it will not lie.*
> *Though it tarries, wait for it;*
> *Because it will surely come,*
> *It will not tarry."*
> *(Habakkuk 2:3)*

Perhaps you are reading this right now and you have lost touch of your youthful dreams, visions, ambitions and aspirations which were birthed in you by God, and it seems you have wasted time, finding it difficult to connect the great future you dreamt of as a teenager with what you are at present; I say to you, don't despair. God gives you hope for restoration. It is time to dream again!

When life's tussles and oppositions confronted Joseph, he dreamt yet another dream (Genesis 37:7-9). When Isaac faced confrontations with his vision of digging a well, he went further and dug yet another well (Genesis 26:18-22). Dream again, beloved! It's never too late to dream again. Conceive another great vision, there is hope for you in God.

The earlier scripture quoted above is actually an excerpt from Acts 2:17. The complete verse reads:

> *"And it shall come to pass in the last days, says God,*
> *That I will pour out of My Spirit on all flesh;*

Your sons and your daughters shall prophesy,
Your young men shall see visions,
Your old men shall dream dreams."
(Acts 2:17)

The outpouring of the Holy Spirit heralds the outcome described. When the Holy Spirit is poured out upon an individual, signifying limitless and bountiful measure of the release of His anointing, the person becomes more and more tuned to the plans and purposes of God for his/her life, for his/her immediate environment, for the nation and for the world at large. Such a person becomes God's ambassador, a representative of God's Kingdom on earth, a witness and bearer of the message of the Gospel (Acts 1:8). God's children are never bereft of great ideas, visions and dreams. They dream dreams and they see visions, young and old alike! That's one of the blessings of redemption!

CHAPTER THREE
Attribute #3: Virtue

"... young men in whom there was no blemish... gifted in all wisdom, possessing knowledge and quick to understand, who had ability to serve in the king's palace, and whom they might teach the language and literature..."
(Daniel 1:4)

Another important attribute of the youth which makes him/her a useful vessel is virtue. Virtue makes a youth exceptional among his/her peers. A virtuous youth has character which adds colour to his candour. Virtue connotes an embodiment of adorable character, comportment and Christlikeness which exemplifies a Christian youth. While some attributes can be observed in all young people, especially vigour and strength, unfortunately virtue is only found in Christ-minded believing youths. That is not to say that some non-Christians do not possess good character, however, in its truest and purest form, virtue is an outflow of the fruit of the Holy Spirit which every believer in Christ has.

In our Bible text above, we found the requirements rolled out for would-be nobles who would serve at the king's palace in Babylon, where the Jews were in exile at that time. Daniel and his three companions were among the Jews in exile who were found to meet, and exceptionally surpass, the requirements and expectations of the king. They were found to be ten times better than the rest of the other candidates! (Daniel 1:19-20).

The enumerated requirements or virtues exhibited by the "Hebrew boys", as they are fondly called in our day, can be categorized into five:

> i. Godliness
> ii. Wisdom
> iii. Skill
> iv. Service
> v. Meekness

Godliness

> *"... young men in whom there was no blemish..."*
> **(Daniel 1:4)**

The first virtue Daniel and his companions showed was Godliness. They were found to be without blemish or anything that defiles. "But Daniel purposed in his heart that he would not defile himself..." (Daniel 1:8). So did his friends.

Godliness is a virtue which flows from a relationship with Jesus Christ. He Himself is God, manifested in the flesh, wholly human in nature yet completely holy, and showed us by example how to live a Godly life, without blemish. Great is the mystery of Godliness! (1 Timothy 3:16). Godliness begins with a decision to know God through faith in the Lord Jesus, then a dedicated followership and obedience to Him follows. For the four Hebrew boys, a determination in their hearts never to defile themselves with whatever they are offered or surrounded with in the "foreign land" where they were exiled, characterized their true faith in God.

To be a useful youth in the hands of God, you must determine not to defile yourself with the things of this worldly system. The Bible classified the blemishes or things of this world that can defile into three: the lust of the flesh, the lust of the eyes, and the pride of life (1 John 2:16). To be a useful vessel in the hands of God, don't attach yourself to the things of the world as though that's all there is. "Don't love the world or the things in the world"(1 John 2:15), the Bible says. Some youths are so overly "in love" with money. Some chase after fame desperately. They want to "blow" and "hammer" quickly. The Bible admonishes that, "Godliness with contentment is great gain." (1 Timothy 6:6). Godliness is a virtue that goes with contentment. Don't let your drive to make earnings drive you into grievous "errings".

Wisdom

> *"… young men … gifted in all wisdom…"*
> **(Daniel 1:4)**

Another distinguishing virtue for a useful youth empowered by God for exploits is wisdom. Impactful youths are men and women of wisdom. They display and exude an endearing exuberance of wisdom, astuteness, insight and intelligence on various matters.

Wisdom is often credited to the old and aged, but impactful and useful youths have a rich store of wisdom. They have the wealth of the old in terms of wisdom. They have the breath of God and therefore commands breadth of knowledge on various key issues as well as depth on matters that matter. Their wisdom makes them dine and whine with nobles and kings. They keep company with sages and they command the attention of the aged. One such youth was Elihu, one of Job's friends (Job 32: 1- 9).

Another Biblical example was Solomon. His wisdom was so well widespread and spoken-of that people, nobles and kings, travelled from far and near, to hear the wisdom of Solomon. Even till now, we read of the wisdom of Solomon in three books of the Old Testament he authored by the inspiration of the Holy Spirit. The Bible wrote of Solomon:

> *"And God gave Solomon a great store of wisdom and good sense, and a mind of wide range, as wide as the sand by the seaside."*
> (1 Kings 4:29, BBE)

Who is the source of such awe-inspiring wisdom? The answer is God. God gave Solomon the wisdom he displayed. Are you wondering if you too can have such wisdom as a youth? The answer is, yes. The Bible encourages us that such a Godly and profound wisdom is possible to have if only you ask:

> *"If any of you lacks wisdom, let him ask of God, who gives to all liberally and without reproach, and it will be given to him."*
> *(James 1: 5)*

Skill

> *"... young men ... possessing knowledge and quick to understand..."*
> **(Daniel 1:4)**

Skill is another virtue useful and purposeful youths possess. Useful youths are skillful, adept and knowledgeable. They add competence to their character which makes them stand out. Impactful youths that command the attention of their generation are youths that have the "knowledge of witty inventions" (Proverbs 8:12, KJV). By virtue of their wisdom, they are committed to acquiring knowledge and skill, making them resourceful and inventive. Daniel and his colleagues displayed this virtue exceptionally well. Another Biblical example worthy of note is David. It was said of David that he shepherded Israel "according to the integrity of his heart, and guided them by the skilfulness of his hands" (Psalms 78:72).

Are you wondering whether or not you could serve God with your professional or secular skills? Is it possible to use your workplace proficiencies in the church? The answer is, yes. If you desire to be useful in the hands of God and in the house of God, you should be willing to deploy all the embodiment of skills, talents, abilities, graces and resources that God has endowed you with, for the service in His Kingdom. That will make you useful and indispensable in His hands! You can be creative about your service in the Kingdom of God.

Service

"... young men ... who had ability to serve in the king's palace..."
(Daniel 1:4)

Service is the hallmark of useful youths. There is no one great person who is not committed to selfless service to God and humanity. If you desire to make a positive impact in life and eternity, you have to choose the path of service. Every great man or woman that has lived has tread this path, and it has delivered its returns in unquantifiable Heavenly rewards. Our Lord Jesus Christ is our perfect Model of a life devoted to service. He lived for God and for the service of mankind. Over 2000 years later and throughout eternity, His name will ever be sung as the Saviour of the world. He enjoined us to follow in His steps.

Embrace service as the goal of life and you will not regret it. Think every day of how you can better the lot of others and you will be well-remembered for good. Don't let only gain motivate you to serve, let the good end of bettering the lot of others, selflessness and Godliness be the motive and drive for your charitable deeds, generosity and kindness. Serve God wholeheartedly wherever God plants you, and make impact for the sake of His Kingdom and not for personal gains. Our Lord Jesus Christ, our perfect example, summarized it thus:

> *"You shall love the Lord your God with all your heart, with all your soul, and with all your mind. This is the first and great commandment. And the second is like it: 'You shall love your neighbor as yourself.' On these two commandments hang all the Law and the Prophets."*
> *(Matthew 22:37-40).*

Love is the motivation for every true and genuine service that is acceptable to God. You must love God wholeheartedly and let that love show by the way you love and treat your neighbour. Love-motivated service is a virtue every true Christian youth on a mission to add value to their generation, is committed to. Are you one of such?

Meekness

"... young men ... whom they might teach the language and literature..."
(Daniel 1:4)

One of the distinguishing attributes of impactful youths who are used by God to create exceptional impact in their time and era is their meekness. Daniel and his companions exhibited this precious virtue in Babylon. They were humble and teachable.

Meekness as a fruit of the Holy Spirit reveals itself as a humble state of the heart, quietness and receptibility to God's instructions, submission to God-ordained authority, and brokenness and sobriety towards God's commandments. Great men of God, patriarchs and saints, who walked with God, are known for their meekness. Meekness endears a man to God.

As a young person on the path to greatness, you must allow the full working of God's Spirit in you to the extent that you cultivate and maintain a meek heart. In today's world, many youths are on frivolous unguided quests and pursuits with haughty motives without the calmness and comportment of a lowly state of heart. Some others lack a teachable attitude pursuing selfish ambitions with indifference to Godly counsel and advice. You shouldn't be like that.

Rather, like the Apostle Paul puts it, you must know how to abound and how to be abased (Philippians 4:12), if you desire to be a youth to reckon with in your day and in your generation. Abound in good works but be abased inwards. Be quick to ascribe accolades to God; be ready to learn and unlearn; and maintain a quiet and teachable heart.

CHAPTER FOUR
Attribute #4: Values

"But also for this very reason, giving all diligence, add to your faith virtue, to virtue knowledge, to knowledge self-control, to self-control perseverance, to perseverance godliness, to godliness brotherly kindness, and to brotherly kindness love. For if these things are yours and abound, you will be neither barren nor unfruitful in the knowledge of our Lord Jesus Christ."
(II Peter 1:5-8)

Purposeful youths on impactful missions are men and women with strong emulatable values. This attribute characterises people of great influence and impact. Your values encapsulate the infallible principles, profound attitudes and personal dispositions that you extol which form the framework for your actions, reactions and behaviour.

Every great achiever has values which guide his/her conduct. They are the tenets they hold dear which they do not give away nor give in to any external influence. They are their formidable character shields which do not collapse no matter the external onslaught of criticisms, derision, mockery or even attack.

Christian Biblical values are age-long, strong, immutable values which have stood the test of time and cannot be eroded by any civilization, culture or criticism. These are the values recommended for any leader, aspiring leader, world changer or influencer, whether young or old. These values are essential add-ons to your Christian virtues.

As a young person who is aspiring to be a great vessel in the hands of God, you need to have a foundational bedrock of solid values which dictate what you watch, what you say, who you relate with and who you listen to. Be careful who you follow. Whose fan are you? Who influences you? What are the values of your so-called "stars" and "idols"? How do they match with yours?

The Bible provides the foundational bedrock of virtues and values for every impact-minded and Heaven-conscious youth. In the opening text for this chapter, we read the inspired words of the Apostle Peter enjoining us to add some key values to our virtues and faith. These key values as listed in the text include:

- Diligence
- Knowledge
- Self-control
- Perseverance
- Godliness
- Kindness
- Love

Diligence

Industry placates poverty. Diligence stands as a sure pathway to durable and enduring affluence and influence. At all times and in any clime, diligence is a proven path to attain greatness. The Bible says, "the hand of the diligent will rule" (Proverbs 12:24). Diligence does not only guarantee good financial success to the youth, in its expression is an embodiment of potent principles capable of liberation and elevation for any youth desirous of making meaningful impact. It is a value that characterises active, proactive and purpose-driven people.

It is an essential add-on to your faith as a Christian youth. Any worthy cause requires diligent hands for it to thrive and make an impact. Youths with emulatable virtues embrace diligence as a candour which adds colour to their sense of calling and mission. No matter how highly-gifted and spiritually sound a man is, if he does not back up his giftedness and spiritual calling with a habit of diligence, industry and hardwork, he might not experience a high level of achievement and fulfillment in his mission. Visions are good, virtues are desirable, vigour is nice to have, but without additional good values like diligence, a man of vision might not experience the visibility and realization of his dreams. The Bible says:

> "Not lagging in diligence, fervent in spirit, serving the Lord."
> (Romans 12:11)

Useful and impactful youths do not lag in diligence. They don't deal with laxity, the mission entrusted into their hands. The proof of your fervency in the Lord and commitment to His service is often how diligent you are in carrying out the tasks and assignments He has asked you to do. Do not join the company of youths who sacrifice diligence for mediocrity and wishful thinking, encouraging laziness over hard work. Embrace diligence as a core value and guard it.

Knowledge

We are at a time in history when knowledge is increasing exponentially. At the click of a button you can find a myriad of information on any subject, good and bad, uncouth, uncensored and uncontrolled. The information age it is called, and the volume of information at our disposal in this age is enormous. As much as it could be enlightening, its enormity is frightening. While the twenty-first century youth has more knowledge at his disposal than a youth of those ancient days, the kind of knowledge he absorbs calls for concern.

Impactful and Godly youths of this age pride not in the knowledge of tech and its kind, they pride in the true knowledge of the Holy One and His Word. The best of knowledge is the knowledge of God and His Son, Jesus Christ. Do you have that knowledge? It is the foundation and bedrock of any meaningful impact.

> *"The fear of the LORD is the beginning of wisdom, and the knowledge of the Holy One is understanding."*
> (Proverbs 9:10)

The knowledge of the Holy One is the most-valuable value you can have. Begin with this, hunger for it, and bequeath it to others! Crave earnestly to know God more, elevate your passion and desire for His Word and His ways, desire to have an unbroken ever-intimate relationship with Jesus, and you can be sure of a life set on the path of glory and greatness. Let your daily quest be like that of the Apostle Paul:

> *"That I may know Him…"*
> (Philippians 3:10)

It's a worthy quest full of great rewards! Invest your time in seeking this kind of knowledge and you would have mastered the secret of good success. Seek God diligently and you will reap Godly rewards for "He is a rewarder of those who diligently seek Him." (Hebrews 11:6).

Self-control

A man who seeks to conquer and influence his world must first learn to conquer himself. To be in control of the resources of this life, you first need to have control over self, for lack of mastery over self makes one a bad master over others. To be a person of impact, you must have your inner self-discipline intact. The Bible enjoins us to discipline our bodies as we engage in the duties of reaching others for God (1 Corinthians 9:27). As a young person, self-control and self-discipline are key values you must guard jealously to protect your integrity and future.

Watch out for the subtle stones which make great men stumble and avoid them. Guard your heart with all diligence (Proverbs 4:23, KJV). Control your appetite for money, fame and romance. These things have brought down great generals in the field at the height of the success of their impactful mission. Beware of the crash which brings down great titans and high-flyers! You must wear self-control as an armour to shield your faith and preserve your character and calling.

Perseverance

In the journey of purposeful and impactful living, there is a value that keeps people of impact tenacious in their pursuits irrespective of the onslaughts of challenges, oppositions and troubles. This value keeps the person of impact focused and on course amidst stormy seas of derailments, discouragements and distractions. Perseverance it is. Every youth on the path of purpose and impact must have perseverance as a vital value to protect them against protracted stormy seasons of life.

The road to prominence and greatness is not always smooth and easy, it is often characterized by bumps, fierce winds and inclement sailing conditions. As a youth on the path of impact and greatness, it is not a question of whether or not there will be storms, it is a question of when the storms do arise, what must you do. You must prepare and persevere. Develop the indispensable value of perseverance and prepare for the boisterous seasons of life.

Perseverance, as a virtue add-on, helps you develop a tough and positive attitude when the challenging situations surface. It helps you to keep your character and develop a formidable survival system. Impactful youths learn to keep their vision, maintain their vigour and preserve their values and virtues, during stormy seasons, through perseverance. It is a valuable add-on to have.

Challenging seasons can turn out to be tests of the things you hold dear. First, the authenticity of your vision is challenged during trying times. Doubts and fears can set in. Raging questions like these often arise: "Am I sure this vision is real?" "Can I actually achieve this task?" "Can this project survive?" In stormy seasons, even your values are not spared the test. They come under serious attack. Imagine going through financial hardships, and you are faced with the temptation of taking from the funds entrusted into your care by your team at church or at work. Or as a young lady with sturdy Christian moral values who is facing imminent expulsion from school due to nonpayment of fees, you meet some man who is offering to help in exchange for sex. These are challenges which test your extolled values and threaten to erode them. But perseverance and a total and complete faith in God can help you steer through these storms and overcome the tests and temptations.

With perseverance, no matter how long your storm lasts, you will always see the light at the end of the tunnel. God will always make a way of escape for you, if you don't cower to your challenges. The Bible says:

> *"No temptation has overtaken you except such as is common to man; but God is faithful, who will not allow you to be tempted beyond what you are able, but with the temptation will also make the way of escape, that you may be able to bear it."*
> (1 Corinthians 10: 13)

Godliness

Godliness features both as an indispensable virtue and value of impactful youths. The subject of Godly living cannot be over emphasized. It is an important requirement that distinguishes persons of lasting impact across ages and dispensations.

Kindness

Another valuable value that characterises people of impact is kindness. It is a distinguishing attribute of people of lasting influence and impact. It is one of the key components in the embodiment of sturdy character and Godly values which make impactful youths people of sound and profound influence. Christian youths fully yielded to God especially display this quality as it is one of the fruits of the Holy Spirit.

Without a heart full of compassion, it is impossible to fashion out a life of success. At the heart of acceptable service is a heart full of compassion. Fulfilment in life is often hinged on the expression of a compassionate heart by intentional acts of kindness. People of impact pay full attention to the needs and feelings of others.

Love

Love caps it all up. Love is the overall and overarching value that sums up all the valuable add-ons the Bible enjoins us to have. It is the foundation and bedrock of all values and virtues displayed by people of meaningful impact. Service without love is empty and valueless. The Bible says:

> "Owe no one anything except to love one another, for he who loves another has fulfilled the law. For the commandments, "You shall not commit adultery," "You shall not murder," "You shall not steal," "You shall not bear false witness," "You shall not covet," and if there is any other commandment, are all summed up in this saying,

namely, "You shall love your neighbor as yourself." Love does no harm to a neighbor; therefore love is the fulfillment of the law." (Romans 13: 8-10)

There are three dimensions of love that every youth aspiring for a life of impact and useful service to God must have. There should be love for God as the primacy and fountain from which all other loves flow from. Secondly, there should be love for others, a category the Bible calls "your neighbour". Lastly, there should be love for oneself. Love for self is necessary because this will also help you to prevent acts and attitudes that may alter your destiny, and it may also serve as a propelling force to attain greatness and fulfill your divine purpose.

CHAPTER FIVE
Attribute #5: Verve

*"Your people will offer themselves willingly...
in the day of Your power;
In the splendor of holiness, from the womb of the dawn,
Your young men are to You as the dew."*
(Psalms 110:3, Amplified)

The Microsoft Dictionary defines verve as "creative enthusiasm, energy, or spirit, especially in the expression of artistic ideas". All young people on the path of a good and laudable mission for God and mankind are characterized by a high spirit of devotion to a worthy cause and willingness to give themselves to its fulfilment. It is not enough to have vigour or strength, a clear vision or dream, worthy emulatable values and virtues, without adding a Godly verve propelling you to action. Men of impact are known to be movers with an inner drive and motivation to accomplish great, laudable and Divine tasks.

Energy, enthusiasm and expression are key components of verve which characterise impactful youths. Add to these, an unparalleled willingness and the propelling Power of the Spirit of God, and you'll have an unstoppable youthful force and voice, capable of transforming the world for the Lord!

Energy

Impactful youths are always in high spirit and their energy is always contagious. It is one of the defining attributes youths are known for. Sometimes, this high-spirited energy reveals itself in ambitious pursuits of goals and life missions. It may manifest in energetic competitiveness with other youths, serving as a driving force for pursuits and accomplishments. Where youths with laudable missions gather, energetic verve, can spring healthy competition for successful accomplishment of ambitions and pursuits.

Enthusiasm

Verve in the purposeful and impactful youth can manifest as enthusiasm and electrifying interest for set-out missions, tasks and goals. Enthusiasm makes an ordinary youth undertake a laudable mission with fervency. The Bible expects this kind of fervency from us, in all matters of service in the Kingdom of God:

> "...not lagging in diligence, fervent in spirit, serving the Lord..."
>
> *(Romans 12:11)*

Expression

When energy and enthusiasm are present as the fuel, the youth is an unstoppable locomotive force jetting off for meaningful impact and expression. Impactful youths are known to be expressive about their convictions and visions; they are like a reverberating voice with a fierce force! They are high-spirited, expressive and full of verve!

Willingness

Increased willingness and desire to do the things of God and be completely sold out to His service is one of the distinguishing features of useful youths with verve, ready for global impact.

In the opening text of this chapter, we read that the "people will be willing in the Day of God's Power". The outflow of youthful revival and fervency is premised on the Power of God in any age and dispensation. The ability of any youthful generation to accomplish great tasks for God and in God is dependent on their willingness to surrender to the move of the Holy Spirit. We are in the end-times and the wave of revival is sweeping across many lands especially among youths on school campuses and church groups. It is sure to be the "Day of God's Power" and there shall indeed be many willing youths passionately driven with the verve of the Holy Spirit for global impact.

CHAPTER SIX
Attribute #6: Valour

"And the Angel of the LORD appeared to him, and said to him, 'The LORD is with you, you mighty man of valor!'"
(Judges 6:12)

In the journey towards a life of impact and positive influence, one additional key attribute is required. It is a distinguishing factor between great achievers and ordinary day-dreamers. It is a quality that makes great visioners become celebrated achievers. Valour is an attribute which helps people of impact to pursue their God-given purpose and vision with dedicated vigour and verve, without the fear of failure or fatigue. In the face of challenges and oppositions, men and women of valour, forge ahead with their vision and goals in mind, with strength of character and courage, until they reach their desired destination or accomplish their set-out mission. People of impact are undoubtedly, men and women of valour whose drive for service to God and humanity propels them to action irrespective of challenges encountered along the way.

Valour does not depend on age or background. The life of Gideon teaches us this. When the Angel of the LORD appeared to him to deliver the message of the LORD and announce God's special assignment for him (the deliverance of the people of God from the hands of the Midianites), Gideon gave excuses why he is not the best candidate for the task. He did not see himself as a mighty man of valour that the LORD called him. His excuses were: "O my Lord, how can I save Israel? Indeed my clan *is* the weakest in Manasseh, and I *am* the least in my father's house." (Judges 6:15).

Your age, position, past or background has nothing to do with the fulfilment of that great mission God has ordained for you. The attribute of valour that God sees and nurtures in you for the accomplishment of that mission is not premised on your inadequacies. Your willingness and complete obedience to God is all that is required.

Valour manifests itself in at least two major ways: courage and confidence. We can see this in the life of Gideon and many other people in the Bible.

Courage

One of the notable manifestations of valour is courage. Men and women of impact are courageous people who are bold to carry out the instructions of God all the time without the fear of people. Joshua, when he was about to take over the leadership of the people of Israel after Moses, was instructed by God to be courageous (Joshua 1:6,7).

Confidence

Confidence in God and His ability is also one of the key drivers of men of valour. The key bedrock of the salutation of the Angel to Gideon in our text is "The LORD is with you, you mighty man of valour". In other words, "Because the LORD is with you, you are a mighty man of valour, Gideon!" The confident assurance of the presence and person of God in one's life is a source of confidence to approach the assignments, visions and goals one set forward to accomplish in life. Men and women of valour do not rely on skills alone; their dependence and reliance is solely on the backing of God, the Giver of strength, resources and results!

As a young person who is desirous of making meaningful impact in life, you must build your confidence only on the Solid Rock, Jesus Christ. Let Him be your Source and Sustainer. The true mighty men are those who have made the Mighty One their All. Greatness emerges for ordinary men who have made the Extraordinary God their Pillar.

CHAPTER SEVEN
Attribute #7: Visible Impact

*"...but the people who know their God shall be
strong, and carry out great exploits."*
(Daniel 11:32)

When all the earlier discussed attributes find their true place in the life of a youth, the seventh attribute of visible impact will manifest as a tangible testimony and outflow of a life of devoted service to God. It is to this end that this book is written that young people everywhere, of all race and creed, will embrace a life full of active and visible proofs of impactful living which better the lot of others thereby making the world a better place. It sets aright the foundation of a glorious life which transcends this earthly realm and guarantees a future life of Heavenly rewards.

The outstanding exploits of Bezalel, Aholiab and other gifted artisans are recorded in Exodus 31:1-11. These men were specially gifted, ordained and anointed by God to design and produce all the "artistic works, in gold, in silver, in bronze, in cutting jewels for setting, in carving wood, in all manner of workmanship" needed for the building of the Tabernacle.

Again, this brings to light the truth that God's gifts in man are meant for God's service no matter how ordinary or seemingly "useless". The Bible says:

> *"Then the LORD spoke to Moses, saying: "See, I have called by name Bezalel the son of Uri, the son of Hur, of the tribe of Judah." (Exodus 31:1-2)*

Who would have thought that "common" artisans would be specially and specifically called by God to attend to important tasks of high spiritual relevance such as designing the artefacts of the Tabernacle including the ark of the Testimony and all the furniture of the Tabernacle? Such is the importance and relevance God places on your gifts, skills and talents no matter how ordinary! When properly surrendered to God, they could be your vehicle to accomplish great exploits for God. Those who know their God, the Source and Giver of their graces and gifts, shall be strong and do great exploits! Welcome to a life of impact!

ABOUT THE AUTHOR

Temitope A. Oshin

Dr. Temitope Alaba Oshin, an engineer and scholar, was born in Lagos, Nigeria. He had his theological training at the Redeemed Christian Bible College, Lagos and professional training at the University of Lagos, Cranfield University and Landmark University.

Temitope uses the avenues of writing and education to reach youths. As a writer, he operates with a mandate from Acts 2:40. He is the Coordinator of Whole Teens Ministries saddled with the mission of raising sons and daughters of God among the teeming generation of young people through the outreach avenues of evangelical writing and publishing, advocacy and enlightenment, educational and empowerment programmes, and evangelical and restorative outreaches.

For pastime, Temitope likes to read biographies, meet and mentor teens, sing and write poems. He is the author of Consecration and Celebration: A Collection of Poems.

BOOKS BY THIS AUTHOR

Consecration And Celebration: A Collection Of Poems

Consecration and Celebration is a collection of heartwarming poems that celebrate the Christian ethos of a devoted and surrendered life. It contains enthusing appreciation of Christ's work at Christmas and Easter for celebration and greetings. Christian character is also praised as you read through some of the collections. The author writes with a call to devotion and dedication.

You will be refreshed, reprimanded, and revived as you read through the poems!

On God's altar I offer my life
I refuse to make a flight
For to work in me His life
To the altar I must stay tight

Though it pains
Yet it pays
For much are the gains
Daily on the altar as I stay

Service offered to Christ
My life and devotion his to have
Till Him I see at last
Forever, Jesus, I'll serve

Made in the USA
Coppell, TX
22 February 2026

71947033R10026